This book belongs to

_____

# COLORS, COLORS EVERYWHERE!

Published by Advance Publishers
Winter Park, Florida

Written by Janet Craig   Edited by Bonnie Brook
Penciled by Len Smith   Painted by Brad McMahon
Designed by Design Five
Cover art by Peter Emslie
Cover design by Irene Yap

ISBN: 1-885222-78-5
10 9 8 7 6 5 4 3 2

It was a bright, sunny day, and Mickey and Goofy were getting ready to paint Mickey's house.

Suddenly Mickey's nephews, Morty and Ferdie, ran in from playing outside.

"May we help you paint, Uncle Mickey?" asked Morty.

"Please?" asked Ferdie.

"Aw, okay," said Mickey. "But first, we need to cover everything in the house with drop cloths."

"You mean everything we don't want painted. A-hyuck!" said Goofy, laughing.

A little while later,
when the furniture was
covered in drop cloths,
Mickey gave Morty
and Ferdie some
red paint for
the kitchen.

Meanwhile, Goofy took some yellow paint
for the hallway.

And Mickey painted the front door blue.

When they had finished, Morty, Ferdie, Mickey, and Goofy met in the living room.

"Let's paint this room purple!" said Morty.

"And the bedroom orange!" said Ferdie.

"And the dining room pink!" said Goofy.

"Gawrsh, we only have red, blue, yellow, black, and white paint," said Goofy.

"Don't worry," Mickey said. "I need gray for the outside of the house, too. I'll just go to the store and get more paint. Goofy, will you watch the boys while I'm gone?"

"Sure thing," said Goofy. "No problem!"

As soon as Mickey was gone, Morty had an idea. "Goofy, may we play tag with Pluto?"

Before Goofy could reply, the two boys were running around the living room, laughing and tagging each other. Pluto barked and barked. Suddenly Morty tripped, tipping over a can of red paint.

Goofy came running behind the boys.
"Whoa!" he said, as he slipped in the
red paint, knocking over the blue
paint. The colors oozed together.
Suddenly, everything
was purple!

Morty and Ferdie ran to the dining room. "I'm tired of tag," said Ferdie. "Let's play ball." Grabbing Pluto's ball, he threw it to Morty. Pluto loved to play catch. He jumped in front of Morty and caught the ball, knocking over a can of white paint!

"Uh-oh!" said Morty. He turned to pick up the can of white paint, but instead knocked over another can of red paint. The red mixed with the white, and soon everything was pink!

"Let's take a ride on the banister!" said Morty.

But as the two boys slid down the railing—*bump!*
They collided with Pluto at the bottom of the
stairs and knocked into a can of yellow paint.

Pluto barked at the boys, who were covered in yellow.
Then the dog ran in a circle and knocked over some blue
paint. It splashed all over Morty and Ferdie. The boys
looked at each other and laughed. They were covered
in green!

"It sure is fun at Uncle Mickey's house," said Ferdie. "What do you want to do next?"

"Let's hide," said Morty, "and see if Goofy can find us!"

The boys heard Goofy coming down the stairs, so they quickly hid.

"Morty! Ferdie!" called Goofy. "Where are you?"

A little voice from somewhere answered, "Come and find us!"

Goofy looked and looked, but he couldn't find the boys. Scratching his head, he said to Pluto, "Gawrsh, where did they go?"

Pluto ran through the house and knocked over a can of white paint near a closet door.

"Oh, no," said Goofy.

"Woof," Pluto barked. When Goofy opened the door to the closet, Morty ran out. In his hurry, he spilled a can of black paint. The white paint and the black paint mixed together. Everything was covered in gray!

Before Goofy could catch
him, Morty shouted, "I'll
help you find Ferdie."

With Goofy behind him,
Morty merrily ran from
room to room. He ended up
in the bedroom, where he
stumbled over a can of red
paint. The paint quickly
covered the floor.

Morty leaned down to get the paint can and saw Ferdie under the bed. "I found you!" Morty cried.

Ferdie laughed and crawled out from under the bed. But as he did so, he tipped over a can of yellow paint. The red and yellow paints ran into each other. Suddenly the floor was orange!

Finally Goofy caught up to them. "Careful, boys!" he said. "We forgot to put a drop cloth on that bed."

It was only then that Morty and Ferdie realized what a terrible mess they had made. Luckily the bed was untouched. But the walls and floors all over the house were covered in paint.

Meanwhile, Mickey had reached the hardware store. He tried to find the colors of paint that the boys wanted, but the store didn't have any.

Sadly, Mickey started
back toward home. He
didn't like to disappoint
Morty and Ferdie. What
could he do?

When Mickey got home, he opened the door.

Pink, purple, green, gray, black, orange, red, yellow, white, blue, and even brown paints were splashed and splattered everywhere.

"What happened?" asked Mickey.

"We're sorry," said Morty and Ferdie sheepishly. "We were playing and spilled the paints. We'll help you clean it up."

Mickey didn't know
what to say or do. He looked at all the colors.

"I guess it's a good thing we covered the furniture
first!" said Goofy.

"Well," said Mickey, "I can't say I'm happy about the
mess, but I am happy about the colors!"

"The colors?" asked Goofy.

Mickey looked around the house. "Yeah, the colors!" he said. "All the colors we wanted are right here!"

"Gawrsh! How did that happen?" asked Goofy.

"It's simple," said Mickey.

"We started out with the colors white, black, red, yellow, and blue. As each of the colors was mixed with another color, a new color was formed. It's like magic."

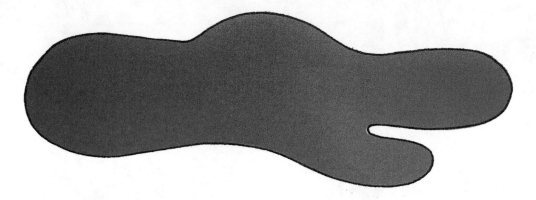

Sure enough, where red and yellow had mixed, there was orange.

Blue and yellow had made green.

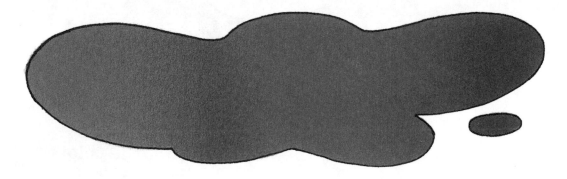

Blue and red had made purple.

White and black had formed gray.

And red and white had made pink.

"There's only one mystery," said Goofy. "Where did this brown color come from?"

"I know," said Ferdie. "All the colors splashed together must make brown!"

"You're right," said Mickey with a smile.

"Now c'mon, guys, help me get more paint from the garage," Mickey said. "We'll mix more colors and paint over some of this mess you've made."

Everyone got busy, carefully stirring different colors together.

The outside of the house
was painted gray.

The dining room was
painted pink.

The bedroom was orange.

And the living room
looked wonderful with its
new coat of purple paint.

When they had finished, Mickey said, "Now there's just one more job to do—clean up!"

First, they carefully took the drop cloths outside.

Then Ferdie
said, "Hey, I've got an
idea. Let's use the hose
to clean ourselves."

They all had fun squirting one
another with the hose. Before long,
they were spotless—and, for once,
Pluto even enjoyed his bath!

They finished just in time to hear the doorbell ring.
It was Minnie. Morty and Ferdie showed her around
the house.

"What colors!" she exclaimed. "You've done a beautiful
job. Your house looks just like a rainbow, Mickey."

"Thanks, Minnie," said Mickey. "I couldn't have done it without the help of my friends and their magic colors."

"Magic colors?" asked Minnie. "What do you mean?"

"Aw," smiled Mickey, winking at Goofy and the boys. "That's just our little secret."